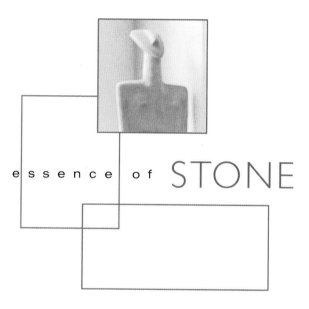

essence of STONE

Hilary Mandleberg

essence of STONE

HarperResource
An Imprint of HarperCollins*Publishers*
www.harpercollins.com

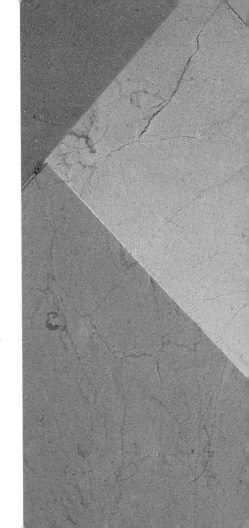

Designer   Luis Peral-Aranda
Editor   Sophie Bevan
Location Research Manager   Kate Brunt
Production   Patricia Harrington
Art Director   Gabriella Le Grazie
Publishing Director   Alison Starling

First published in Great Britain in 2000
by Ryland Peters & Small

ESSENCE OF STONE
Text copyright © Hilary Mandleberg 2000
Design and photographs copyright
© Ryland Peters & Small 2000

Library of Congress Cataloging-in-Publication
Data available on request
ISBN 0-688-17434-5

10 9 8 7 6 5 4 3 2 1

Printed and bound in China by
Toppan Printing Co.

contents

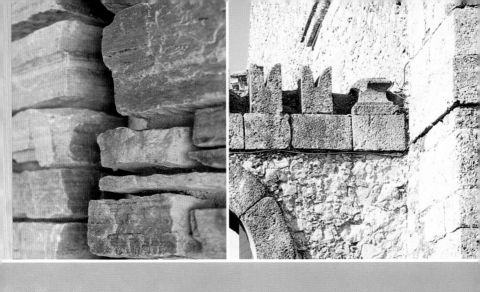

shelter

Everywhere it is found, stone expresses solidity, permanence, the power of nature, and a sense of nobility—a combination possessed by no other organic building material.

From paleolithic times to the twenty-first century, stone has provided us with shelter and sanctuary. Ancient caves bear witness to the lives of our earliest ancestors. Later came tools and temples of stone that testified to the permanence of the gods, and

ROCK OF AGES

stone-built fortifications and palaces to consolidate the power of rulers. Marvel today at the work of ancient Greeks, Romans, Egyptians, Aztecs, and Incas. Wonder at the art of the Renaissance or the beauty of the Taj Mahal and know that stone is eternal.

The ancient architects did not have a monopoly on the use of stone. Early in the twentieth century, Edward Lutyens was the height of refinement with his stone-covered English country houses, while Frank Lloyd Wright's low-built prairie-style homes display the beauty

BACK TO THE FUTURE

of rough-hewn stone. Concrete was the darling of the Modern movement, but Le Corbusier, Breuer, and Gropius all used stone, too. And in recent years, Richard Meier and even Frank O. Gehry have chosen stone facings for a timeless and classical look.

shades & textures

Stone blends with the land from which it comes, a fact that has not escaped even the earliest architects' notice. Each type is formed differently, hence their differences of strength, color, texture, and composition. Sandstone and limestone are the sedimentary

NATURAL CUNNING

stones, formed by the compression of layers of mud and fossils in old sea and river beds. Their colors are generally beige, cream, and almost-white. Sandstone has a high silica content, which gives it its sparkle, while in limestone, you can often see remains of shells and fossils. Granite is the best-known of igneous rocks, formed when the earth's molten crust

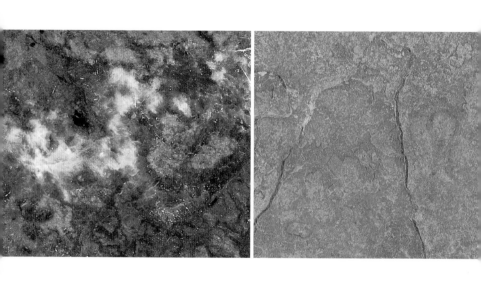

cooled, over 500 million years ago. Ranging from black to gray through shades of red, green, and blue, it is

immensely strong and hard to work.
Marble and slate are the metamorphic
rocks—rocks changed through heat or

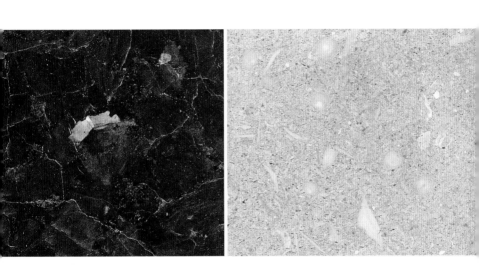

pressure: marble from recrystallized
limestone, slate from clay-rich rocks
under pressure for millions of years.

Limestone and marble are relatively easy to cut and shape, making them suitable for use as bathtubs and sinks. Polishing brings out the detail.

Stone's many shades and textures make it perfect in combination with other materials. Always regarded as

something of a luxury—marble was often imitated by painting onto wood—happily, you only need to use it sparingly. An exquisitely veined and detailed marble fireplace or an old weathered garden ornament stand on

their own as classics. But stone takes a different turn alongside rough-cast concrete or a crisp white linen towel.

Stone is the frame on which the earth is modeled and wherever it crops out—there the architect may sit and learn.

Frank Lloyd Wright

living spaces

Not so long ago, with the exception of flagstones and cobblestones, stone was the preserve of the wealthy. Now, thanks to fast, cheap transportation, it comes from all over the world and is within the reach of many. It is so versatile you can use it in any room,

LIVE LIKE A LORD

but durability and easy maintenance make it a great choice for heavy-wear areas like halls and kitchens. And although it is noisy and cold—try underfloor heating—those drawbacks are outweighed by stone's dramatic qualities and simple elemental beauty.

The slate on this staircase can only have been laid by a professional. In areas like this, there is no furniture to distract from the sheer enjoyment this fine, natural material can bring.

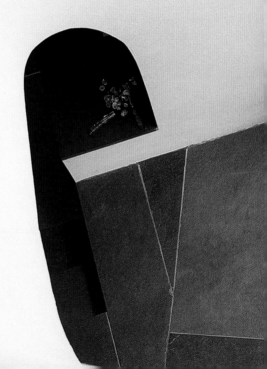

Stone can look sleek, expensive, and urban, or cozy, homey, and rustic. The trick often lies in how it is cut and finished. Urban architects love to use gleaming rectangles or squares, while irregular, unpolished shapes speak of the country. Different types of stone

DRESS TO IMPRESS

also suit different locations, but it is fun to break the rules. Slate and pebbles are at home in the country, but try using them in a defiantly metropolitan apartment and enjoy the culture clash. Pebbles set in concrete bridge the divide between urban and

rural, while split stones partner wood
to perfection. Traditional or modern,
in the kitchen, marble and slate rule.

At home in bathrooms since the days
of the Romans, stone is a must for
indulgent bathing. Site bathtubs and
sinks on top of stone or set them
underneath; but why stop there? Use

granite for shelves. Take marble up the walls. Lay limestone or slate over the floor. Finally, fill your bathtub with bubbles, lie back, and enjoy stone's classic elegance.

ornament

You may not be able to replace your living-room carpet with slate or your laminated work surfaces with granite, but you can introduce stone into your house on a smaller scale—as a bowl, a shelf, a rough boulder, or a collection of pebbles picked up on a beach. Such

PASTORAL IDYLL

stone details are a means of bringing nature into the modern environment, where the emphasis is usually largely on machine-made artifacts. Stone makes reference to the outdoors in the same way that a pastoral painting would in a loft apartment.

In the not-so-distant past, when stone was used as ornament in rich men's houses—and they would have had to be very rich—it was for classical decorative details such as pillars and columns, cornices and moldings, fireplaces and marble flooring. Then,

VANITY OF VANITIES

stone was used as much to proclaim wealth and importance as for its own inherent beauty. The ultimate vanity would be to have a marble statue of yourself—Roman-emperor style—in the main reception room of your home. Nowadays, stone ornaments can be for all. We take it far less seriously and enjoy it in the home for what it is. In contemporary design, it is often the

details and how you place them that give pleasure. Stone is perfect for this fresh new approach. Left just to its own devices, a stone object can evoke the grandeur of a past age or the simplicity of a rustic kitchen. It

can conjure up an image of a stroll along a mossy riverbank or can evoke the spirituality of the single standing stones that meant so much to our forefathers. Used on a grand scale, stone ornament will always be a way of saying, "Look at me, I'm rich," but it can just as easily decorate a table

for simple outdoor eating or form part of a collection of found objects with no value to anyone other than the owner. Now—rich or not-so-rich—we can all enjoy stone in our homes.

outside

Stone started life outdoors, formed millennia ago by movements of the earth's crust and by intense heat and pressure deep in its core, so it is no surprise that it looks handsome in an outdoor setting. It harmonizes with the landscape to a degree that modern

BORN TO BE WILD

materials, like concrete or glass, never will, and it grows old (or should one say older?) beautifully, just like antique furniture. Doesn't it look as if a piece of weathered stone is trying to return to the earth from where it came? Perhaps it never really left.

Decorating the yard with stone is hardly a new idea. The Romans certainly did it, with marble statues, urns, columns, and pools, while in the Renaissance, the art reached a peak. Today's look is freer and not so formal. Local volcanic stones pave an orange-painted concrete courtyard. A simple stone spout gushes into a plain stone basin. A pool of water lies peacefully in its stony surround. Or why not enjoy stone outside just as nature intended—simply sitting on a windswept pebble beach?

credits

Architects and designers and useful addresses

Key: **a**=above, **b**=below, **l**=left, **r**=right, **t**=telephone, **f**=fax, **ph**=photographer

Claire Bataille & Paul ibens Design
NV Architects
Vekestraat 13 Bus 14
2000 Antwerpen
Belgium
t. 00 32 3 231 3593
f. 00 32 3 213 8639
Pages 30, 40–41, 48

Ann Boyd Design Ltd
33 Elystan Street
London SW3 3NT
UK
t. 00 44 20 7591 0202
Page 8

L.B.D.A.
Laura Bohn Design Associates
30 West 26th Street
New York, NY 10010
t. (212) 645 3636
Page 29 r

Alastair Hendy
Food writer, art director, and
designer
f. 00 44 20 7739 6040
Pages 42, 44

Hudson Featherstone Architects
49–59 Old Street
London EC1V 9HX
UK
t. 00 44 20 7490 5656
Pages 32–33, 47

Campion A. Platt Architect
641 Fifth Avenue
New York
NY 10022
t. (212) 355 360
Page 36

Guiseppe Prato
Architect
t. 00 39 95 375 261
Page 6

Mark Pynn A.I.A.
McMillen Pynn Architecture L.L.P.
P.O. Box 1068
Sun Valley, Idaho 83353
USA
t. (208) 622 4656
f. (208) 726 7108
e. mpynn@sunvalley.net
w. www.sunvalleyarchitect.com
Pages 29 l, 37

Jonathan Reed
151a Sydney Street
London SW3 6NT
UK
t. 00 44 20 7565 0066
f. 00 44 20 7565 0067
Page 28

Johanne Riss
Stylist, designer, and fashion
designer
35 Place du Nouveau Marché aux
Gräens
1000 Brussels
Belgium
t. 00 32 2 513 0900
f. 00 32 2 514 3284
Page 46

Sally Storey
John Cullen Lighting
585 King's Road
London SW6 2EH
UK
t. 00 44 20 7371 5400
Page 28

SCDA Architects
10 Teck Lim Road
Singapore 088386
t. 00 65 324 5458
f. 00 65 324 5450
e. scda@cyberway.com.sg
Pages 27 inset, 58–59

Hervé Vermesch
50 rue Bichat
75010 Paris
France
t. 00 33 42 01 39 39
Page 39

José de Yturbe
De Yturbe Arquitectos
Patriotismo 13 (4° piso)
Lomas de Barrilaco
Mexico 11010 DF
t. 00 525 540 368
f. 00 525 520 8621
Page 56

photographers

Front cover main ph Andrew Wood; **Front cover inset ph** Henry Bourne; **Back cover ph** Pia Tryde; **Spine ph** Fritz von der Schulenburg; **Front flap ph** Andrew Wood; **Back flap ph** Andrew Wood; **1 ph** Henry Bourne; **2 ph** Andrew Wood; **3 ph** Henry Bourne; **6 ph** Simon Upton; **7 l ph** Andrew Wood; **7 r ph** Simon Upton; **8 ph** Simon Upton; **9 ph** Andrew Wood; **11 ph** Simon Upton; **12–13 ph** Andrew Wood; **14 ph** Andrew Wood; **16 ph** Henry Bourne; **17 l ph** Henry Bourne; **17 r ph** Simon Upton; **18 ph** Simon Upton; **19 ph** Fritz von der Schulenburg; **20–23 ph** Henry Bourne; **24 l ph** Fritz von der Schulenburg; **24 r ph** Andrew Wood; **25 l** Henry Bourne; **25 r ph** Stephen Robson; **26–27 main ph** Andrew Wood; **27 inset ph** Andrew Wood/Isosceles Land Pte Ltd's house in Singapore designed by Chan Soo Khian of SCDA Architects; **28 ph** Ray Main/Jonathan Reed's apartment in London, lighting designed by Sally Storey, Design Director of John Cullen Lighting; **29 l ph** Andrew Wood/Philip and Barbara Silver's house in Idaho designed by Mark Pynn A.I.A. of McMillen Pynn Architecture L.L.P.; **29 r ph** Ray Main/an apartment in New York designed by Laura Bohn Design Associates Inc., light from Lightforms; **30 ph** Andrew Wood/House near Antwerp designed by Claire Bataille & Paul ibens; **32–33 ph** Henry Bourne/a house in Devon designed by Hudson Featherstone Architects; **34 ph** James Merrell; **36 ph** James Merrell/an apartment in New York designed by Campion A Platt Architect; **37 ph** Andrew Wood/ Phil and Gail Handy's house in Idaho designed by Mark Pynn A.I.A. of McMillen Pynn Architecture L.L.P.; **38 ph** James Merrell/Consuelo Zoelly's apartment in Paris; **39 ph** James Merrell/an apartment in Paris designed by Hervé Vermesch; **40 ph** Andrew Wood; **40–41 ph** Andrew Wood/House near Antwerp designed by Claire Bataille & Paul ibens; **42 ph** Andrew Wood/Alastair Hendy and John Clinch's apartment in London designed by Alastair Hendy; **43 l ph** James Merrell; **43 r ph** Sandra Lane; **44 ph** Andrew Wood/Alastair Hendy and John Clinch's apartment in London designed by Alastair Hendy; **46 ph** Andrew Wood/Johanne Riss' house in Brussels; **47 ph** Simon Upton/a house in Devon designed by Hudson Featherstone Architects; **48 ph** Andrew Wood/House near Antwerp designed by Claire Bataille & Paul ibens; **50 l ph** Simon Upton; **50 r ph** Sandra Lane; **51 l ph** James Merrell; **51 r ph** Fritz von der Schulenburg; **52–53 ph** Tom Leighton; **54 ph** Andrew Wood; **55 l ph** Pia Tryde; **55 r ph** Simon Upton; **56 ph** Simon Upton/José de Yturbe; **58–59 ph** Andrew Wood/Isosceles Land Pte Ltd's house in Singapore designed by Chan Soo Khian of SCDA Architects; **60–61 ph** Tom Leighton; **62–64** Henry Bourne; **Endpapers ph** Pia Tryde.

The author and publisher would also like to thank all those whose homes or work are featured in this book.